American Moments

ABDO
Daughters

SEPTEMBER 11, 2001
By Alan Pierce

VISIT US AT
WWW.ABDOPUB.COM

Published by ABDO Publishing Company, 4940 Viking Drive, Suite 622, Edina, Minnesota 55435. Copyright © 2005 by Abdo Consulting Group, Inc. International copyrights reserved in all countries. No part of this book may be reproduced in any form without written permission from the publisher. ABDO & Daughters™ is a trademark and logo of ABDO Publishing Company.

Printed in the United States.

Edited by: Melanie A. Howard
Interior Production and Design: Terry Dunham Incorporated
Cover Design: Mighty Media
Photos: AP/Wide World, Corbis, Library of Congress

Library of Congress Cataloging-in-Publication Data

Pierce, Alan, 1966-
   September 11, 2001 / Alan Pierce.
      p. cm. -- (American moments)
   Includes index.
   ISBN 1-59197-735-5
   1. September 11 Terrorist Attacks, 2001--Juvenile literature. 2. Terrorism--United States--Juvenile literature. 3. Terrorism--History--Juvenile literature. I. Title. II. Series.

HV6432.7.P54 2004
973.931--dc22

                                   2004052163

CONTENTS

How Can It Happen? 4

A History of Terrorism 6

Arabs and Israelis 10

Iran, Afghanistan, and Lebanon 16

The Rise of al Qaeda 22

Targeting the United States 26

A Nation Under Attack 32

Defending America 38

Timeline 42

Fast Facts 44

Web Sites 45

Glossary 46

Index 48

HOW CAN IT HAPPEN?

On the morning of September 11, 2001, people going to work noticed an alarming sound. In New York City, they heard a jet engine that sounded closer than it should be. Then, people in Manhattan witnessed a horrifying sight. A jet crashed into the north tower of the World Trade Center.

People inside the 110-story skyscraper were jolted by the impact. The building shook and windows vibrated. Workers inside the building scrambled to leave, but dust and smoke hindered their escape. Eventually, many people managed to make their way to the street. A scene of calamity met those who had escaped from the tower. Debris and paper from the tower's offices lay scattered on the ground.

Several minutes later, another airliner hurled into the south tower of the World Trade Center. Some who saw the second jet strike the tower immediately thought it was a terrorist attack. People now began to run from the area. A little later, many people stopped to look at the damaged twin towers.

They did not have long to look. Soon, the south tower began to collapse, sending up a column of smoke. Clouds of dust rolled through the streets, driving New Yorkers before it. More than 20 minutes later, the north tower also tumbled down and again dust

United Airlines Flight 175 flies into the south tower of the World Trade Center. The north tower is already in flames.

filled the streets. After the second tower collapsed, a witness asked, "How can it happen in America?"

Since September 11, 2001, Americans have struggled with the question of how the attacks could have happened. But they also have learned some information as well. They found out that 19 Middle Eastern terrorists had hijacked four passenger jets. Two flew into the World Trade Center towers, and a third struck the Pentagon in Arlington, Virginia. A fourth crashed in a field in Pennsylvania. More than 2,900 people died in these attacks. The United States had experienced terrorist attacks before, but never any that were so devastating.

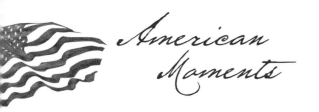

A HISTORY OF TERRORISM

The September 11, 2001, terrorist attacks shocked people in the United States and the rest of the world. But violence associated with terrorism has existed for centuries. More than 2,000 years ago, the Greek writer Xenophon discussed terrorism. He suggested psychological warfare be used against a hostile population.

Later, Roman emperors used cruel methods to suppress those who challenged their power. These practices included exile and execution. The Roman Empire also slaughtered foreign civilians to terrify its foes.

Tribes that invaded the Roman Empire also committed violence against civilians. The Huns had a fierce reputation in Europe in the fourth and fifth centuries. They were masterful horsemen who killed both soldiers and civilians.

In the thirteenth century, the Mongols also caused destruction throughout Asia and parts of Europe. They slew both warriors and civilians in their conquests. The Mongols cared very little about the difference between civilians and warriors. This was simply how they fought.

Another group practiced terrorism in the thirteenth century. The Nizari Isma'ilites murdered their political opponents in the Middle East. Members of this Islamic group were called *hashshash* or *hashshashin*. The word *assassin* comes from the name of this violent group.

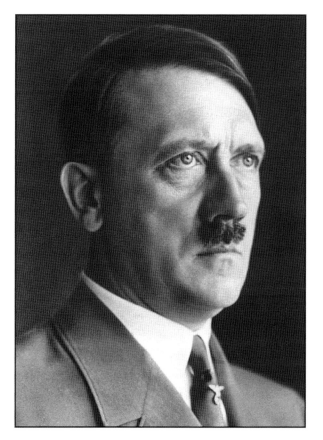

Adolf Hitler

Joseph Stalin

Within the last two centuries, the meaning of terrorism began to mean a specific kind of violence. Terrorism became associated with violence that a government committed against its own people. During the French Revolution, the people suffered through a period known as the Reign of Terror. Between 1793 and 1794, France's revolutionary government killed thousands of people who were considered a threat to the Revolution. This violent phase helped give rise to the word *terrorism*.

In the twentieth century, some governments continued to terrorize their populations. Two examples are Adolf Hitler's Germany and Joseph Stalin's Soviet Union. Both governments killed, tortured, and imprisoned their own citizens. These governments committed this violence to intimidate people into obeying the government. The people had no legal protection against this brutality.

More recently, terrorism has become harder to define. One problem is that terrorism is often hard to distinguish from other forms of violence. Some experts have proposed ways of thinking about terrorism, though. For example, terrorists have political goals, and they use violence to achieve them. Terrorism can be thought of as violence committed by a group to produce a climate of fear. The group hopes this fear will compel the government to yield to the group's demands.

The violence carried out by terrorists is different from the violence committed by a nation's armed forces. Both armies and terrorists fight opponents. But armies use the strength of their weapons to force enemies to surrender. Terrorists lack the resources to fight their enemies directly. Instead, terrorists try to create a sense of fear among people through the use of violence.

Terrorism also differs from conventional warfare in another important way. In war, there are certain international rules. For example, military forces are not supposed to take civilians hostage. Also, military forces are prohibited from attacking civilians. Militaries sometimes break these rules. However, when violations occur, international and national courts can punish these offenders.

Terrorists do not abide by the rules of war. They take civilians hostage and target civilians for death. Moreover, they often attack places with large numbers of people such as schools, restaurants, and train stations. By attacking places where people expect to feel safe, terrorists heighten the sense of fear.

Terrorism can be committed by foreigners or by a country's own citizens. Domestic terrorism occurs when a nation's citizens attack their own country. An example of domestic terrorism occurred in the

After a terrorist attack, crews remove debris from the Alfred P. Murrah Federal Building in Oklahoma City, Oklahoma.

United States on April 19, 1995. A bomb inside a rental truck exploded outside the Alfred P. Murrah Federal Building in Oklahoma City, Oklahoma. The explosion killed 168 people and wounded more than 500 others. Former U.S. soldiers Timothy McVeigh and Terry Nichols were charged with the bombing.

The attacks on September 11, 2001, were examples of foreign terrorism. This is because the attacks were committed by people who were not U.S. citizens. Most of the 19 hijackers were Saudi, while the rest were Egyptian or Yemeni.

ARABS AND ISRAELIS

Many people throughout the world have used terrorism to further their causes. In Ireland, a group called the Irish Republican Army (IRA) has existed since 1919. It seeks to unify Northern Ireland with the Republic of Ireland. Since the 1920s, Northern Ireland has remained part of the United Kingdom, which includes England, Scotland, and Wales. England has been the target of many IRA attacks. In recent years, peace talks have curbed violence in Northern Ireland.

Terrorist groups operate in many other places besides Ireland. In Spain, the Euzkadi Ta Azkatasuna (ETA) formed in 1959. This organization wants a separate nation for the Basque people living in Spain. Japan has also faced terrorist groups such as AUM Shinrikyo. This religious group believed it would rule Japan after a disaster occurred. In 1995, members of AUM released nerve gas in the subway in Tokyo, Japan. The attack killed 12 people and injured thousands.

Although terrorism occurs throughout the world, it has become identified with the Middle East. The phrase *Islamic terrorism* is often used to refer to Middle Eastern terrorists. The religion of Islam, however, should be distinguished from terrorism.

The majority of the people living in the Middle East are Muslims. A Muslim is someone who follows the religion of Islam. The word

Opposite page: *A boy in Madrid, Spain, protests against the ETA after a car bomb explosion near a department store.*

Islam means "surrender" in Arabic. Those who practice Islam are expected to submit to God's will. Muslims and Arabs are sometimes seen as being the same people. Arabs are people who speak Arabic as a native language. While most Arabs are Muslims, some Arabs do practice religions other than Islam.

The book called the Koran offers the most important teachings in Islam. Muslims believe the Koran contains the word of God. According to Muslims, the angel Gabriel revealed God's message to the prophet Muhammad. The revelations began in the seventh century and took place over several years. These revelations formed the Koran.

Muhammad's life was closely connected to two cities in present-day Saudi Arabia. He was born in Mecca and his tomb is in Medina. These two cities are the holiest places in Islam. The Great Mosque is located in Mecca. Muslims face this city when they pray five times a day. Also, each Muslim is called upon to make a pilgrimage to Mecca at least once during his or her lifetime.

The conflict between Arabs and the Jewish state of Israel has led to much of the strife in the Middle East. In the late nineteenth and early twentieth centuries, Jews wanted to escape the hostility they faced in Europe.

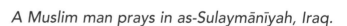

A Muslim man prays in as-Sulaymānīyah, Iraq.

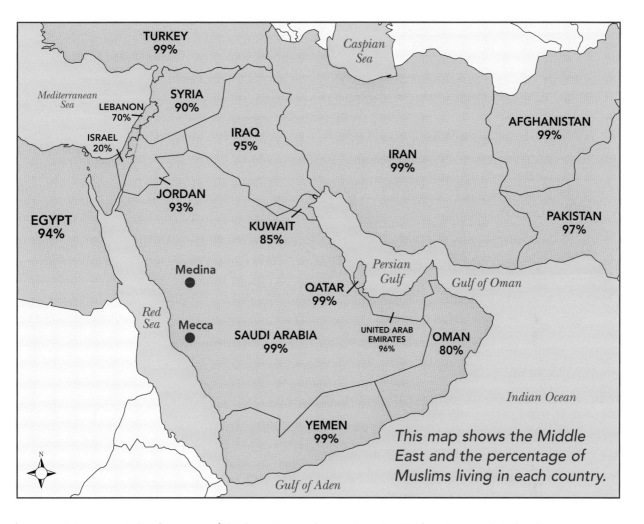

Many wished to establish a Jewish nation in Palestine, which the Jews considered to be their homeland. Thousands of Jews arrived in Palestine to settle. Arabs in Palestine were worried these immigrants would make Palestine into a Jewish state.

In the 1940s, Britain controlled Palestine, but both Arabs and Jews wanted their independence. Jewish residents formed terrorist groups such as the Irgun Zvai Leumi to attack the British and the Arabs. On July 22, 1946, Irgun Zvai Leumi exploded a bomb at a site were British offices were located. The blast at the King David Hotel in Jerusalem killed 91 people, including soldiers and civilians. Eventually, Britain decided to let the United Nations (UN) oversee Palestine.

In 1947, the UN approved a settlement. The Jews and the Arabs would each receive a nation in Palestine. Arabs, however, were angry about the decision. Nevertheless, on May 14, 1948, Israel declared its independence. The announcement provoked an invasion from the surrounding Arab countries. Egypt, Iraq, Lebanon, Syria, and Jordan all attacked Israel.

Israel received foreign help and managed to fend off the Arab armies. But another problem developed. The war left more than 600,000 Palestinian Arabs homeless. They were forced to live in other Arab countries and in refugee camps.

Over the next several years, Palestinian terrorist groups dedicated to fighting Israel began to emerge. Many came together to form the Palestine Liberation Organization (PLO) in 1964. It worked toward the destruction of Israel. By the late 1960s, members of the PLO began waging guerrilla warfare against Israel. In the early 1970s, Jordan expelled the PLO. The group then moved to Lebanon.

Another Palestinian terrorist group formed in response to the PLO's removal from Jordan. This group was called Black September. These terrorists attacked Jordanian officials and committed terrorist acts in Israel.

The Black September group carried out its most shocking attack at the 1972 Summer Olympics in Munich, West Germany. Terrorists murdered two Israeli athletes. Nine other Israelis were taken hostage. In exchange for the hostages, the terrorists demanded the release of Arab prisoners being held by Israel. However, Israel refused to negotiate.

Later, the hostages and five of the terrorists were killed in a gunfight at an air base. A police officer also died in the shoot-out. The Germans later captured the remaining terrorists. That fall,

German police officers in Munich, Germany, drop onto the terrace above the apartments where Black September terrorists are holding nine Israeli athletes hostage.

other Black September terrorists hijacked a West German airliner. They threatened to blow up the plane if the captured terrorists were not released. West Germany released the terrorists. However, Israel is believed to have killed most of the terrorists who were freed.

In the 1980s, other groups began to attack Israel. One group called Hezbollah began fighting Israeli forces after Israel invaded Lebanon in 1982. Hezbollah was also accused of carrying out terrorist attacks against Americans and Europeans.

Religious members of the PLO and other Islamic activists started another organization in 1987. This group is called Hamas. It seeks to replace Israel with an Islamic state. Hamas has carried out several suicide bombings in Israel.

IRAN, AFGHANISTAN, AND LEBANON

While Israel has many enemies, it also receives abundant help. The United States provides Israel with billions of dollars each year in military and economic aid. The two countries have had a close relationship. Both are democracies, and Israel enjoys strong support in the U.S. Congress.

The United States' friendship with Israel, however, has a drawback. Arabs are angry about American support for Israel. For many Arabs, this support is their biggest criticism of the United States. Israelis use helicopters and weapons obtained from the United States to fight Palestinians. Arabs who see Palestinian casualties on television become angry at the United States.

Others see the conflict between the United States and Arab countries as a clash of cultures. American television shows, music, and fast food are available in Arab nations. Arab societies tend to be more traditional and place a strong emphasis on religion. Some Arabs view the presence of American culture as threatening and offensive.

Religion has also been identified as playing a role in the conflict between the United States and Muslims who commit terrorism. Some have suggested that terrorists follow a misguided form of Islam.

16

Israeli prime minister Ariel Sharon meets with U.S. president George W. Bush

A few Muslim leaders have promoted the idea of killing the enemies of Islam. If terrorists die in the process, they become martyrs. According to this belief, the terrorists see Americans as infidels, or nonbelievers. It is then the obligation of the terrorists to kill Americans.

There is another reason for the unpopularity of the United States in Arab countries. The United States supports many governments in the Middle East that do not grant their people much freedom. Although some Arab countries have allowed democratic reforms, many Arab governments generally do not tolerate opposition. Many of these Arab countries encourage criticism of the United States to deflect anger away from their own governments.

The United States supports many of these governments anyway because they provide some stability in the Middle East. Order is important in the Middle East because this region supplies much of the world's oil. Oil is critical for the U.S. economy and military.

Oil has both benefited and hampered Middle Eastern countries. Nations that produce oil have become extremely wealthy. But the wealth generated by oil has not spread to everyone in these countries. Consequently, poverty still exists in these areas.

Many of America's problems in the Middle East can be seen in the relationship between Iran and the United States. Iran is an important oil-producing country. Mohammad Reza Pahlavi, the shah of Iran, was a longtime ally of the United States. Although he implemented many social reforms, he did not tolerate opposition to his government. His secret police, known as Savak, tortured and killed many of those who opposed him.

One of the shah's greatest opponents was Ayatollah Ruhollah Khomeini. He was a Shiite leader who the shah had exiled. In 1979,

Ayatollah Ruhollah Khomeini

A poster of Khomeini

Ruhollah Musawi was born sometime around the year 1900 in Khomein, Iran. He later took the name of his birthplace as his last name. His father and grandfather were both mullahs, or religious leaders, in the Shiite sect. Khomeini followed in their footsteps.

In the early 1960s, Khomeini spoke out against the corrupt rule of Mohammad Reza Pahlavi, the shah of Iran. He objected to the shah's land reforms because they took land away from religious groups. Khomeini also opposed the shah's policy to give women more rights.

After the shah was overthrown, Khomeini returned to Iran as the country's leader. He established a theocracy, or religious government, based on Islam. Khomeini remained a political leader until his death on June 3, 1989.

a revolution forced the shah to leave Iran. Khomeini became head of the new Iranian government. He criticized the United States for its support of the shah and called the U.S. government the "Great Satan."

In October 1979, the shah entered the United States for medical treatment. On November 4, Islamic militants seized the U.S. embassy in Tehran, Iran, with Khomeini's approval. They took more than 60 Americans hostage. The militants demanded the return of the shah for the hostages. In response, the United States quit importing Iranian oil and froze $8 billion in Iranian assets. Later the Iranians released some hostages, but still held 52 Americans.

Meanwhile, the Soviet Union had become entangled in Afghanistan, a country that borders Iran. Afghanistan's leader, Nur Mohammad Taraki, was friendly toward the Soviet Union. But in 1979, Taraki's enemies murdered him. In December 1979, the Soviet army invaded Afghanistan and installed Babrak Karmal as the leader.

Some U.S. officials thought the Soviets intended to move toward the oil fields in the Middle East. President Jimmy Carter was convinced the invasion signaled a threat. He declared that the United States would use military force to defend its interests in the Persian Gulf.

The United States, however, already had its own problems. The Iranian hostage crisis continued to be a maddening experience. In April 1980, the military conducted a mission to free the hostages. The rescue attempt ended in disaster when an airplane and a helicopter collided in the Iranian desert. President Carter's popularity continued to drop because of the Iranian hostage crisis and a troubled U.S. economy. In November, he lost the 1980 presidential election to Ronald Reagan.

By now, Iran also faced a major problem. Iraq had launched a surprise invasion of Iran. This made the U.S. hostages less important to Iran. Eventually, the United States and Iran reached an agreement. Iran turned over the hostages and the United States agreed to release Iran's assets. The hostages were freed on January 20, 1981.

The resolution of the Iranian hostage crisis did not end the troubles for the United States in the Middle East. The United States

President Jimmy Carter

The U.S. embassy in Beirut, Lebanon, following a truck bomb explosion

became involved in Lebanon, which was caught up in the conflict between Israel and the PLO. U.S. troops and soldiers from other nations tried to restore order to the country.

Lebanon, however, remained a violent place. This was made clear on April 18, 1983. A terrorist with a truck full of explosives crashed into the U.S. embassy in Lebanon's capital, Beirut. The explosion killed 63 people, including 17 Americans. Hezbollah was blamed for the attack.

The United States suffered a greater calamity on October 23, 1983. A truck bomb exploded at the U.S. Marine barracks at the Beirut International Airport. The blast killed 241 marines and injured more than 100 other marines. Hezbollah was again suspected of the attack, but the United States was unsure. Four months later, the United States pulled the marines out of Beirut.

THE RISE OF AL QAEDA

The Soviets were facing their own disaster in Afghanistan. The Soviet Union had committed more than 100,000 troops to the war. In addition, the Soviets also bombed the country's villages and countryside. But a great number of people in Afghanistan resisted the Soviet occupation. These fighters were called *mujahideen*.

For many Muslims, the war against the Soviets was a *jihad*. The word jihad is an Arabic term that means "struggle" or "battle." It is often translated as meaning "holy war." Jihad has been used in the past to describe wars against people who are not Muslims. Today, Islam is more likely to refer to jihad as a struggle with one's self to do what is right. Violence is only recommended when the Islamic faith is at stake.

The Afghans received help from other countries, including the United States. In 1986, the United States began to provide Stinger missiles to the Afghan resistance. These missiles allowed the Afghans to shoot down low-flying aircraft and helicopters.

Others also contributed to Afghanistan's struggle against the Soviet Union. An unknown number of Muslims journeyed to Afghanistan to drive the Soviets out of an Islamic country. Among them was a man named Osama bin Laden.

Bin Laden was a Saudi man, although neither of his parents was originally from Saudi Arabia. His father, Muhammad Awad bin Laden,

Opposite page: *Osama bin Laden*

was a Yemeni man who moved to Saudi Arabia in the 1930s. In Saudi Arabia, Muhammad Awad bin Laden became wealthy in the construction business. Osama bin Laden's mother, Hamida, was from Syria. She was one of Mohamed Awad bin Laden's many wives. Osama bin Laden was born in 1957.

When Osama bin Laden was 11 years old, his father died in a helicopter crash. After his father's death, bin Laden inherited millions of dollars. Later, he attended King Abdul Aziz University in Jidda, Saudi Arabia. He studied management and economics. He also studied Islam.

Soon after the Soviet invasion, bin Laden went to Afghanistan to aid the anti-Soviet resistance. There he met a Jordanian Palestinian named Abdullah Azzam. They established an organization called the Afghan Service Bureau. This group recruited and trained Arab and Muslim fighters. In addition, bin Laden used his wealth and construction ties to help the anti-Soviet cause. He brought equipment to Afghanistan to build roads and tunnels.

As the war continued, a split developed between Azzam and bin Laden. Many of the Arab fighters in Afghanistan wanted to spread the armed struggle. They wanted to topple the oppressive governments in their own countries. Azzam disagreed with this goal, while bin Laden approved of the idea. In the late 1980s, bin Laden began setting up training camps for his own fighters. These trained fighters became the basis of al Qaeda, which is Arabic for "the base."

Meanwhile, another source of Middle Eastern terrorism troubled the United States. Throughout the 1980s, the United States and Libya had a hostile relationship. The Reagan administration was furious about Libya's support of terrorism. In 1986, a bomb killed

The 747 airliner destroyed over Lockerbie, Scotland,
was also known as the Clipper Maid of the Seas.

two U.S. soldiers and wounded 229 people in West Berlin in East Germany. The United States blamed Libya for the attack. A few days later, U.S. warplanes bombed Libya.

On December 21, 1988, another terrorist attack occurred when Pan Am Flight 103 exploded over Lockerbie, Scotland. The explosion killed all 259 people on the plane and another 11 on the ground. Authorities later accused Libyan intelligence agents of planting a bomb aboard the airplane. The United States and Britain demanded that Libya turn over two people accused of carrying out the attack. Libya eventually granted the request.

TARGETING THE UNITED STATES

A new crisis was emerging in the Arab world. Iraq was in bad economic shape after its war with Iran. Iraq had borrowed money from Kuwait to finance the war. On August 2, 1990, Iraqi president Saddam Hussein ordered his army to invade the oil-rich nation of Kuwait in order to obtain control of Kuwait's resources.

By this time, the Soviet Union had withdrawn its troops from Afghanistan. Osama bin Laden had returned to Saudi Arabia where he was considered a hero. He wanted to use the mujahideen to drive the Iraqis out of Kuwait. The Saudi government turned down bin Laden's offer. Instead, Saudi Arabia accepted help from the United States, which sent thousands of troops to Saudi Arabia. From bases in Saudi Arabia, U.S. troops could launch an offensive against Iraq. This conflict became known as the Persian Gulf War.

The United States was joined by several allies, including Britain, France, Egypt, Saudi Arabia, and Syria. On January 16, 1991, the United States and its allies launched a bombing campaign against Iraqi targets. More than a month later, the United States and its allies followed up with a ground attack that drove the Iraqis out of Kuwait.

After the war, U.S. troops remained in Saudi Arabia. These forces were stationed there to enforce the southern no-fly zone in Iraq. The United States and its allies established the zone to protect Iraq's

ECOTERRORISM

In the photo above, Kuwaiti oil wells are in flames. When the Iraqi military retreated from Kuwait during the Persian Gulf War, it set these oil wells on fire. This caused massive environmental damage. This kind of action is known as ecoterrorism.

Ecoterrorism has also been called ecological terrorism and environmental terrorism. This kind of terrorism occurs when an individual, group, or government destroys or threatens to destroy some part of the environment. Ecoterrorists hope that this destruction will scare civilians or governments into giving in to the terrorists' demands.

An example of ecoterrorism occurred during the Vietnam War in the 1960s and 1970s. The United States used a chemical mixture called Agent Orange to defoliate the jungles where the enemy could hide. In 1976, the United Nations (UN) banned actions during war that caused serious and long-term damage to the environment. The UN later made ecoterrorism a war crime.

Shiite population in the southern part of the country. Iraq was not permitted to fly aircraft in this area.

The presence of foreign troops angered bin Laden. He considered these soldiers to be infidels. Their presence was especially offensive to bin Laden because they occupied the country where Mecca and Medina are located. He began plotting to rid Saudi Arabia of foreign troops.

Meanwhile, another terrorist named Ramzi Ahmed Yousef planned an attack against the United States. The target was the World Trade Center. It is unknown whether or not Yousef was connected to bin Laden. However, Yousef was known to have contacts with Sheikh Omar Abdel Rahman. In Egypt, Rahman had started a terrorist group dedicated to overthrowing the government. He later led a mosque in New Jersey.

On February 26, 1993, Yousef and others exploded a bomb in the basement garage of the north tower of the World Trade Center. The blast killed 6 people and injured more than 1,000. About 50,000 people were forced to leave the trade center complex.

It is believed that Yousef hoped to destroy both towers by having the north tower fall on the south tower. Yousef's bomb failed to topple the building, but it did produce a crater five stories deep. Later, Yousef was charged in connection with the bombing and sentenced to life in prison.

By this time, bin Laden had returned to Afghanistan. In that country, he supported a group called the Taliban. This organization took its name from the Persian word for students. The Taliban had started out as Islamic students in Afghan refugee camps. But by September 1996, Taliban forces had captured the Afghan capital of Kabul. The Taliban eventually controlled most of the country.

$2,000,000
REWARD

At approximately 12 noon on February 26, 1993, a massive explosion rocked the World Trade Center in New York City, causing millions of dollars in damage. The terrorists who bombed the World Trade Center murdered six innocent people, injured over 1,000 others, and left terrified school children trapped for hours in smoke filled elevators.

Following the bombing, law enforcement officials obtained evidence which led to the indictments and arrests of several suspected terrorists involved in the bombing. RAMZI AHMED YOUSEF, one of those indicted, fled the United States immediately after the bombing to avoid arrest. YOUSEF is now a fugitive from justice. YOUSEF was born in Iraq or Kuwait, possesses Iraqi and Pakistani passports, and also claims to be a citizen of the United Arab Emirates. Because of the nature of the crimes for which he is charged, YOUSEF should be considered armed and extremely dangerous.

The United States Department of State is offering a reward of up to $2,000,000 for information leading to the apprehension and prosecution of YOUSEF. If you have information about YOUSEF or the World Trade Center bombing, contact the authorities, or the nearest U.S. embassy or consulate. In the United States, call your local office of the Federal Bureau of Investigation or 1-800-HEROES1, or write to

HEROES
Post Office Box 96781
Washington, D.C. 20090 – 6781
U.S.A.

RAMZI AHMED YOUSEF
DESCRIPTION

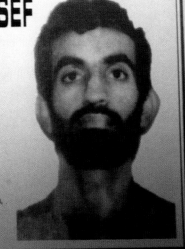

DATE OF BIRTH: May 20, 1967 and/or April 27, 1968
PLACE OF BIRTH: Iraq, Kuwait, or United Arab Emirates
HEIGHT: 6'
WEIGHT: 180 pounds
BUILD: medium
HAIR: brown
EYES: brown
COMPLEXION: olive
SEX: male
RACE: white
CHARACTERISTICS: sometimes is clean shaven
ALIASES: Ramzi A. Yousef, Ramzi Ahmad Yousef, Ramzi Yousef, Ramzi Yousef Ahmad, Ramzi Yousef Ahmed, Rasheed Yousef, Rashid Rashid, Rashed, Kamal Ibraham, Kamal Abraham, Abraham Kamal, Muhammad Azan, Khurram Khan, Abdul Basit.

Wanted poster for Ramzi Ahmed Yousef issued after the 1993 bombing of the World Trade Center in New York City, New York.

Taliban rule greatly affected the population. Women were required by law to wear veils. Moreover, women were shut out from employment and education. People caught stealing had their hands or feet cut off. Taliban leaders also outlawed television because they considered it a form of Western corruption.

During this time, bin Laden urged Muslims to attack the United States. He delivered this message in fatwas, or religious opinions. Bin Laden's chief complaint against the United States was the presence of U.S. troops in Saudi Arabia. He accused the United States of "occupying the lands of Islam in the holiest of its territories."

Soon after bin Laden's declaration of war, the United States came under attack in Africa. On August 7, 1998, bombs severely damaged the U.S. embassies in Tanzania and Kenya. The bomb in Nairobi, Kenya, killed 291 people and wounded more than 4,000. In Dar es Salaam, Tanzania, the blast killed 10 people and injured more than 70.

Al Qaeda and bin Laden were soon blamed for the attacks. President Bill Clinton ordered a response to the embassy bombings. On August 20, U.S. Navy ships fired cruise missiles into Afghanistan and Sudan. The United States intended to destroy an al Qaeda training camp in Afghanistan. Missiles were fired at a factory in Sudan because the United States believed the plant made materials for chemical weapons. The U.S. government claimed that bin Laden was involved with the factory, but this was not proven.

The cruise missile failed to stop al Qaeda from engaging in terrorism. In fact, some authorities think al Qaeda leaders began to plan the September 11, 2001, attacks at about this time. A few of the men who would hijack the airliners lived in Hamburg, Germany. In 2000, three of these men moved to Florida, where they took flight lessons.

A Kenyan soldier raises the U.S. flag for a memorial service honoring those who died in the U.S. embassy bombing.

But al Qaeda was also doing more than planning terrorism. The group was carrying out attacks. On October 12, 2000, the navy destroyer USS *Cole* sustained major damage in the port in Aden, Yemen. A dinghy rigged with explosives ran into the ship, killing 17 crew members and injuring 42. U.S. and Yemeni officials investigated the attack and arrested al Qaeda suspects, who later escaped.

A NATION UNDER ATTACK

In 2001, the rest of the men who would participate in the hijackings arrived in the United States. No one is certain where the men would have practiced the hijackings. But it is possible that the hijackers might have trained at one of al Qaeda's camps in Afghanistan. By 2001, more than 15,000 people from Muslim countries are believed to have trained at these camps.

In the summer of 2001, there were indications of potential terrorists attacks that might involve airplanes. An agent for the Federal Bureau of Investigation (FBI) in Phoenix, Arizona, alerted the agency about an investigation. Agent Kenneth Williams was investigating Middle Eastern men who were taking flight training in Arizona. Williams raised the possibility that Osama bin Laden might want pilots. He also suggested that the FBI check the visa applications of Middle Eastern men who were in flight training.

None of the men Williams investigated turned out to have connections to terrorism. However, another man in flight training also aroused suspicions. This man's name was Zacarias Moussaoui. He was born in Morocco, but was a

FBI agent Kenneth Williams

ZACARIAS MOUSSAOUI

Police photo of Zacarias Moussaoui

Zacarias Moussaoui was born on May 30, 1968. Before coming to the United States, Moussaoui attended a terrorist training camp in Khalden, Afghanistan. In late February 2001, Moussaoui trained at Airman Flight School in Norman, Oklahoma. He did poorly in that program. In August 2001, Moussaoui attended flight school in Eagan, Minnesota. Flight instructors at this school alerted the FBI about Moussaoui's suspicious behavior.

At first, the FBI believed that Zacarias Moussaoui was slated to be another hijacker on September 11, 2001. Officials now believe that Moussaoui may have been preparing to be part of a second wave of terrorist attacks.

French citizen. Moussaoui had possible links to al Qaeda, but U.S. authorities did not know this. He took pilot training lessons in Eagan, Minnesota, near Minneapolis. He was vague about his background, which concerned a flight instructor.

Soon, someone at the flight school reported Moussaoui to the FBI. On August 15, agents questioned Moussaoui. They gave custody of Moussaoui to the Immigration and Naturalization Service because he had violated his visa.

FBI agents wanted to search Moussaoui's computer. However, FBI headquarters in Washington DC never gave the agents permission to do so. Unfortunately, the agents investigating Moussaoui were not aware of Williams's warning to the FBI. And Williams was not aware that Moussaoui had been taken into custody.

On September 10, members of al Qaeda were staying in hotels in the United States. The next day, the 19 men boarded planes at different airports. Five al-Qaeda members boarded American Airlines Flight 11 at Logan International Airport in Boston, Massachusetts. Five other members got on United Airlines Flight 175 at the same airport. At Dulles International Airport in Washington DC, five more al Qaeda members boarded American Airlines Flight 77. Only four al Qaeda members went on United Airlines Flight 93 at Newark Airport in Newark, New Jersey.

The terrorists on all four flights managed to hijack the jets. At 8:46 AM, Flight 11 flew into the north tower of the World Trade Center. A little after 9:00 AM, Flight 175 crashed into the south tower. Workers in the towers fled the calamity, but thousands of others rushed to the scene. Those who arrived were firefighters, police officers, and other rescue workers. When the towers collapsed, 479 of these rescue workers died.

On this day, President George W. Bush was at Emma E. Booker Elementary School in Sarasota, Florida. He was reading to students and promoting his education program. At 9:05 AM chief of staff Andrew Card whispered into Bush's ear. A few minutes later, the president left to talk to his advisers.

At 9:30 AM, the president made an announcement in the elementary school's library. He said an "apparent terrorist attack" had occurred. But he assured the country that "Terrorism against our nation will not stand." Afterward, the president went to Sarasota Airport where Air

White House chief of staff Andrew Card informs President George W. Bush that a second plane has hit the World Trade Center.

Force One was waiting. He flew to Barksdale Air Force Base in Shreveport, Louisiana.

At about this time, Flight 77 flew into the southwest side of the Pentagon. The jet tore through three of the building's rings. All 59 passengers aboard the jet were killed and another 125 people died in the Pentagon.

Meanwhile, Flight 93 proceeded south. The situation aboard this flight was different from the other hijacked airliners. Passengers had talked to their families by cell phones. These passengers knew the hijackers were not negotiating to achieve a certain outcome. Instead, the hijackers were crashing planes into buildings.

Based on the cell phone calls, it appears the passengers struck back. A telephone supervisor heard one passenger, Todd Beamer, say, "Are you guys ready. Let's roll." The uprising kept the plane from damaging or destroying another national symbol. No one is certain, but the White House or the U.S. Capitol are considered the plane's likely targets. Flight 93 crashed into a field near Shanksville, Pennsylvania. All 45 people aboard were killed.

After these staggering events, President Bush addressed the country from Barksdale Air Force Base. He said the U.S. military had been put on high alert. Moreover, Bush vowed to pursue those behind the attack. Later, the president flew to Offutt Air Force Base near Omaha, Nebraska.

That evening, President Bush returned to the White House. There, he delivered an address to the nation. "These acts of mass murder were intended to frighten our nation into chaos and retreat. But they have failed. Our country is strong. A great people have been moved to defend a great nation."

The terrorist attacks on September 11, 2001, did move the nation. Americans were shocked and outraged by the loss of life. But the attacks also inspired patriotism. People flew flags and donated money to the Red Cross and other relief organizations. Retired firefighters went to New York to help with the recovery effort.

Opposite page: *President George W. Bush addresses the nation on the evening of September 11, 2001.*

DEFENDING AMERICA

The U.S. government suspected bin Laden and al Qaeda of carrying out the attacks. Some Americans took out their anger on Arabs and Muslims living in the United States. Arab Americans and Muslims reported being threatened. In some cities, police were called in to protect mosques with additional patrols. President Bush asked Americans to treat Arabs and Muslims with respect.

The president also increased efforts to catch bin Laden, who was in Afghanistan. Bush demanded that the Taliban turn bin Laden over to the United States. The Taliban refused, and the United States waged a war to overthrow the Afghan leadership.

U.S. Special Forces entered Afghanistan in October. They worked with a group called the Northern Alliance. Ethnic groups opposed to the Taliban made up these fighters. In addition, the United States used its warplanes to bomb Taliban forces. By December, the United States and the Northern Alliance had defeated the Taliban. However, bin Laden had escaped. U.S. troops searched for bin Laden in the mountains between Afghanistan and Pakistan.

The United States also took action to fight terrorism at home. In July 2002, the United States created the Department of Homeland Security. This government agency strives to prevent terrorist attacks and to protect the country's borders.

Two women listen to a poem entitled "9-11-01"
during a memorial service in St. Paul, Minnesota.

Airport security also came under scrutiny after September 11. The airlines implemented greater safety procedures at airports. More thorough checks of passengers also created longer lines.

The United States also formed a committee to investigate the September 11, 2001, terrorist attacks. The National Commission on Terrorist Attacks Upon the United States, is better known as the 9-11 Commission. One of the commission's duties is to make recommendations to prevent more terrorist attacks.

In the wake of September 11, the United States has made plans for memorials. These monuments will honor the victims at all three sites of the terrorist attacks. The memorial at the World Trade Center will feature two reflective pools where the towers once stood. The names of those killed will appear around the pools. This memorial will honor those who died in the 1993 and 2001 terrorist attacks at the World Trade Center.

Plans are also underway to construct the world's tallest building at the site. The skyscraper will stand 1,776 feet (541 m) and be topped by a 276-foot (84-m) spire. The height of the skyscraper symbolizes the year 1776 when the American colonies declared their independence. New York governor George Pataki has called the building the "Freedom Tower."

Another memorial will honor the 184 lives lost at the Pentagon. A park on the west side of the Pentagon will include 184 aluminum markers among 70 maple trees. These markers will serve as benches and feature the names of the victims.

Those who died aboard United Airlines Flight 93 will also be honored. Thousands of people have visited the Pennsylvania crash site since September 11, 2001. They have left many flowers, messages, and other items at a nearby temporary memorial. Congress has approved legislation to create a permanent memorial there.

The efforts to fight al Qaeda and terrorism have not yet ended in a victory over terrorists. Al Qaeda remains capable of violence. For example, authorities blamed al Qaeda for bombings that killed 190 people in Madrid, Spain, on March 11, 2004. On the other hand, police have prevented terrorist attacks. In May 2004, police announced that they stopped a planned terrorist attack in Istanbul, Turkey.

Experts continue to debate whether the United States is making progress in the war against terrorism. Some claim that al Qaeda has been significantly weakened. Others say the United States needs to do more. In any case, those who study terrorism do not expect this type of violence to disappear any time soon.

Bruce Fraser hangs a picture of his sister on a wooden angel at the temporary memorial for United Airlines Flight 93.

TIMELINE

1948 On May 14, Israel declares its independence. Israel fends off an attack from neighboring Arab nations.

1964 The Palestine Liberation Organization (PLO) is established.

1972 A terrorist group called Black September kills 11 Israeli athletes at the Summer Olympics in Munich, Germany.

1979 In December, the Soviet Union invades Afghanistan to establish a friendly government. Soon, Osama bin Laden travels to Afghanistan to help drive out the Soviets.

1979 to 1981 On November 4, 1979, Islamic militants seize the U.S. embassy in Iran. The militants hold 52 hostages until January 20, 1981.

1983 On April 18, the terrorist group called Hezbollah bombs the U.S. embassy in Beirut, Lebanon.

On October 23, the U.S. Marine barracks in Beirut are also bombed. Hezbollah is suspected.

Late 1980s Bin Laden forms the al Qaeda terrorist group in Afghanistan.

1990 to 1991 On August 2, 1990, Iraq invades Kuwait and refuses to withdraw, triggering the Persian Gulf War. The United States and its allies attack Iraq, forcing the Iraqis to retreat from Kuwait.

1993 On February 26, a terrorist named Ramzi Ahmed Yousef explodes a bomb in the basement of the north tower of the World Trade Center, killing six people.

1995 On April 19, Timothy McVeigh and Terry Nichols explode a bomb outside the Alfred P. Murrah Federal Building in Oklahoma City, Oklahoma, killing 168 people.

1996 In September, the Taliban takes control of Kabul, and later most of Afghanistan.

1998 On August 7, al Qaeda explodes bombs at the U.S. embassies in Dar es Salaam, Tanzania, and Nairobi, Kenya. The United States responds by bombing suspected al-Qaeda targets in Afghanistan and Sudan on August 20.

2000 The U.S. Navy ship USS *Cole* is bombed on October 12. Al Qaeda suspects are captured, but later escape.

2001 On September 11, four airplanes are hijacked by al Qaeda terrorists. Two planes are flown into the World Trade Center twin towers in New York City, New York, causing both towers to collapse. Another of the four planes is flown into the Pentagon in Washington DC. The fourth plane crashes in a field near Shanksville, Pennsylvania, after passengers fought for control of the plane.

American Moments

FAST FACTS

The collapse of the World Trade Center towers was measured by equipment that record earthquakes. Equipment at Columbia University in New York City detected the force of the planes hitting the towers and their collapse. Scientists said the collapse released more energy than a small earthquake that hit New York City in January 2001. The earthquake measured 2.4 on the Richter scale

The youngest victim of the September 11, 2001, attacks was two-year-old Christine Hanson. Robert Grant Norton, 85, was the oldest victim. Both were passengers on the hijacked airplanes that flew into the World Trade Center.

It took 108,342 truckloads to remove the almost 1,641,000 tons (1,489,000 T) of debris that remained of the twin towers. Crushed office equipment, pieces of airplane fuselages, and other unearthed items have ended up in a traveling exhibit and in the Smithsonian.

Sales of the American flag increased dramatically in the week following September 11, 2001. One U.S. flag maker produced ten times the usual number of flags in the week after the attacks.

The states of New York and New Jersey lost the most people on September 11, 2001. New York victims numbered more than 1,700, and New Jersey lost more than 700 people. Among the victims, more than 35 states are represented. Victims also came from 12 other nations and one U.S. territory.

WEB SITES
WWW.ABDOPUB.COM

Would you like to learn more about September 11, 2001? Please visit **www.abdopub.com** to find up-to-date Web site links about September 11, 2001, and other American moments. These links are routinely monitored and updated to provide the most current information available.

Firefighters walk toward the twin towers through dust and smoke.

GLOSSARY

assassin: one who murders public figures.

asset: something of value. When a government freezes assets, it is stopping the production of the assets.

calamity: an event marked by death and a period of suffering.

casualty: something or someone that is lost or destroyed.

civilian: a person who is not a member of the military.

cruise missile: a low-flying guided missile that has a radar system.

custody: to have control or possession of someone.

democracy: a governmental system in which the people vote on how to run their country.

dinghy: a small sailboat, rowboat, or life raft.

embassy: the home and office of a diplomat who lives in a foreign country.

exile: to force people to leave their country.

guerrilla warfare: a kind of fighting where a small group of militants combat the enemy with sudden attacks.

hijack: to overtake a vehicle, such as an airplane, by threatening the pilot with violence.

hostage: a person being held against his or her will by a criminal who wants to make a deal with authorities.

martyr: a person who voluntarily dies for the sake of a principle.

mosque: a Muslim place of worship.

prophet: a religious leader who speaks as the voice of God.

psychological warfare: using tactics that will disturb the mind of one's enemy and make them lose their will to fight.

refugee camp: a camp for people who have been displaced from their homeland.

revelation: truth revealed to one by God.

sect: a small religious group that holds differing beliefs from the majority.

shah: the title of a ruler in Iran.

Shiite: a member of the second largest group of Muslims, the Shia. Shiites follow the leadership of the descendants of Muhammad's son-in-law, Ali.

suicide bombing: a bombing in which bombers deliberately blow themselves up along with their target.

visa: a document that is added to foreigners' passports that gives them permission to be in the country.

INDEX

A

Afghanistan 19, 20, 22, 24, 26, 28, 30, 32, 38

American Airlines Flight 11 34

American Airlines Flight 77 34, 35

Azzam, Abdullah 24

B

Beamer, Todd 36

bin Laden, Osama 22, 24, 26, 28, 30, 32, 38

Britain 10, 13, 25, 26

Bush, George W. 34, 36, 38

C

Carter, Jimmy 20

Clinton, Bill 30

D

Department of Homeland Security 38

E

Egypt 9, 14, 26, 28

F

Federal Bureau of Investigation (FBI) 32, 33, 34

G

Germany 7, 14, 25, 30

H

Hamas 15

Hezbollah 15, 21

I

Iran 18, 19, 20, 26

Iraq 14, 20, 26

Islam 6, 10, 12, 15, 16, 18, 19, 22, 24, 28, 30

Israel 12, 14, 15, 16, 21

J

Japan 10

Jordan 14, 24

K

Karmal, Babrak 20

Khomeini, Ayatollah Ruhollah 18, 19

Kuwait 26

L

Lebanon 14, 15, 21

Libya 24, 25

M

McVeigh, Timothy 9

Mecca, Saudi Arabia 12, 28

Medina, Saudi Arabia 12, 28

Moussaoui, Zacarias 32-34

N

National Commission on Terrorist Attacks Upon the United States 39

New York City, New York 4, 36, 40

Nichols, Terry 9

Northern Alliance 38

O

Oklahoma City, Oklahoma 9

P

Pahlavi, Mohammad Reza (shah of Iran) 18, 19

Palestine 13, 14, 16, 24

Palestine Liberation Organization (PLO) 14, 15, 21

Pan Am Flight 103 25

Pataki, George 40

Pentagon 5, 35, 40

Q

Qaeda, al 24, 30, 31, 32, 33, 34, 38, 40

R

Rahman, Omar Abdel 28

Reagan, Ronald 20, 24

S

Saudi Arabia 9, 12, 22, 24, 26, 28, 30

Shanksville, Pennsylvania 36

Soviet Union 19, 20, 22, 24, 26

Spain 10, 40

Sudan 30

Syria 14, 24, 26

T

Taliban 28, 30, 38

Taraki, Nur Mohammad 19, 20

U

United Airlines Flight 93 34, 35, 36, 40

United Airlines Flight 175 34

United Nations (UN) 13, 14

USS *Cole* 31

W

Washington DC 33, 34

Williams, Kenneth 32, 34

World Trade Center 4, 5, 28, 34, 39, 40

Y

Yemen 9, 24, 31

Yousef, Ramzi Ahmed 28